Taffy was a Welchman, Taffy was a thief, Taffy came to my house, + stole a

"Hark, Hark, the Dogs

Hark, hark, the dogs do bark, The beggars are coming to town,

Dance.

"Butter Scotch"
Highland Fling

Lively

"Butter Scotch"
Highland Fling

Lively

The Lancer's Quadrille

J. S. KNIGHT

LA DORSET

Play eight bars prelude before commencing the figure

Taffy was a Welchman.

Taffy came to my house, + stole a piece of beef, I went to Taffy's house, Taffy wasn't home, I return
a w

Hark, the Dogs do bark."

gars are coming to, town, Some in rags, + some in tags, + some
and some in

Taffy was a Welchman.

Taffy came to my house, + stole a piece of beef, I went to Taffy's house, Taffy was'nt home, I retu
a

"Hark, the Dogs do bark."

ggars are coming to, town, Some in rags, + some in tags, + some
and some in

English Country Dance

English Country Dance

Hungarian Dance
No 6.

J. BRAHMS

Hungarian Dance
No 6.

J. BRAHMS

Mexican Hat Dance
Jarabe Tapatio

F. A. PARTICHELA

Allegro

Mexican Hat Dance
Jarabe Tapatio

F. A. PARTICHELA

Allegro

Old Time Waltz Medley

THE MAN ON THE FLYING TRAPEZE

BOWERY

Old Time Waltz Medley

THE MAN ON THE FLYING TRAPEZE

BOWERY

เพลงชาติ

บทร้องไทย ขุนวิจิตรมาตรา ทำนองไทย พระเจนดุริยางค์

บทร้องไทย นายฉันท์ ฉันทวิไล

เหล่าเราทั้งหลาย, ขอน้อมกาย, ถวายชีวิต.
รักษาสิทธิ์, อิสสระ, ณแดนสยาม,
ที่พ่อแม่, สู้ยอมม้วย, ด้วยพยายาม,
ปราบเสี้ยนหนาม, ให้พินาศ, สืบชาติมา,
แม้ถึงไทย, ไทยด้อย, จนย่อยยับ,
ยังกู้กลับ, คงคืน, ได้ชื่นหน้า,
ควรแก่นาม, งามสุด, อยุธยา,
นั้นมิใช่ว่า, จะขัดสน, หมดคนดี,

เหล่าเราทั้งหลาย เลือดและเนื้อ, เชื้อชาติไทย
มิให้ใคร, เข้าเหยียบย่ำ, ขยำขยี้
ประคับประคอง, ป้องสิทธิ์, อิสสระเสรี
เมื่อภัยมี, ช่วยกัน, จนวันตาย
จะสิ้นชีพ, ไว้ชื่อ, ให้ลือลั่น
ว่าไทยมั่น, รักชาติ, ไม่ขาดสาย
มีไมตรี, ดียิ่ง, ทั้งหญิงชาย
สยามมิวาย, ผู้มุ่งหมายเชิดชัย ไชโย

เพลงชาติ

บทร้องไทย ขุนวิจิตรมาตรา　　　　　　　ทำนองไทย พระเจนดุริยางค์

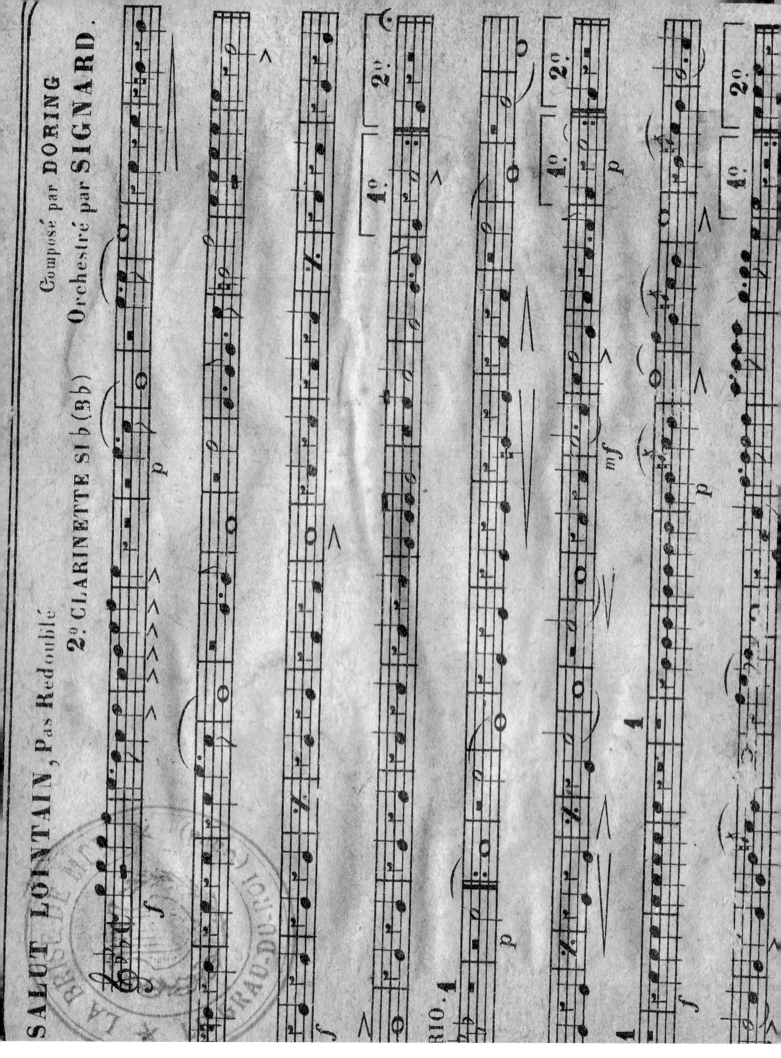

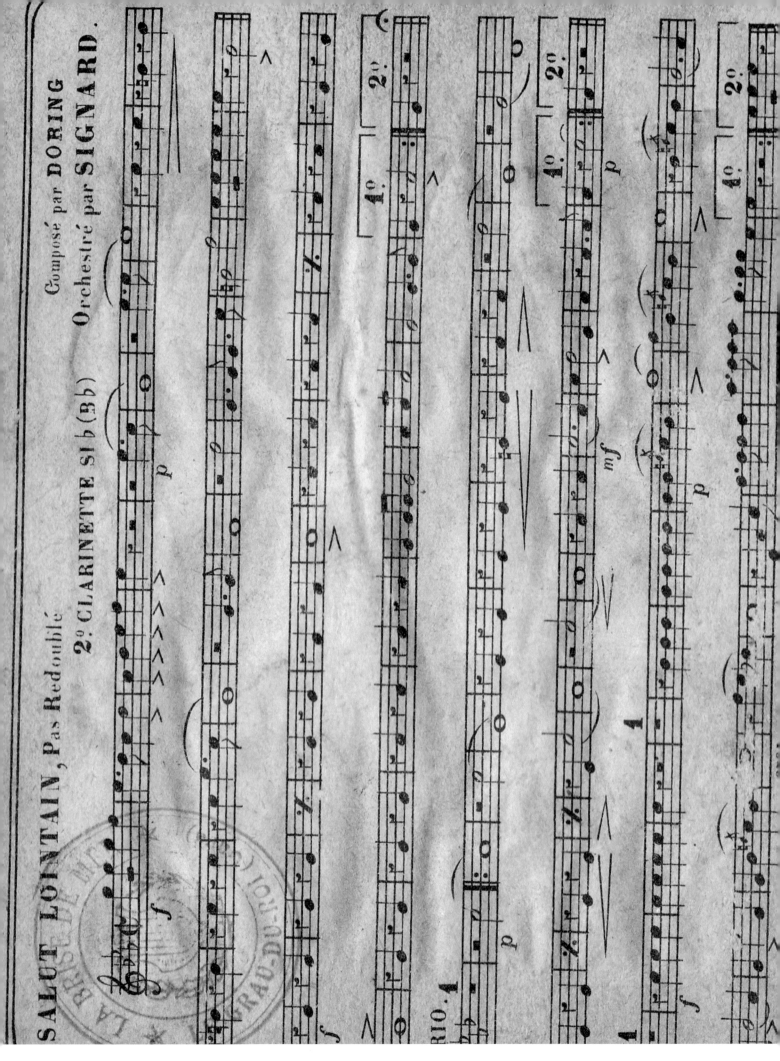

Composé par DORING

Orchestré par SIGNARD.

SALUT LOINTAIN, Pas Redoublé

2.º CLARINETTE SI b (Bb).